Choose a topic and start to practise writing. Each booklet has a theme to help you start to write…stories, reports, articles, letters and many more. Start collecting them now.

Guinea Pig creative writing booklets also provide extra practice for children who have completed:

- Creative Story Writing ISBN: 9780955831508
- Persuasive Writing & Argument ISBN: 9780955831515
- Information Writing ISBN: 9780955831522

They are for:

* children who are working at Key Stage 2 of the National Curriculum, levels 3-5 (in Years 5 and 6 of primary school),
* children who are working at Key Stage 3, levels 3-5 (Years 7 and 8 of Secondary School).

They provide practice for all 9-13 year olds, especially children taking 11+ examinations.

Written by Sally A Jones and Amanda C Jones

Published by GUINEA PIG EDUCATION

2 Cobs Way,
New Haw,
Addlestone,
Surrey,
KT15 3AF.

www.guineapigeducation.co.uk

First things first...
Let's **learn** to *write* <u>fiction</u>.

When you *write fiction*, <u>**you must**</u>:

1. Decide who will be your audience?

2. Think of different genres – realistic, detective, ghost, gothic horror.

3. Ask what is the purpose of my writing?

When you *write to entertain*, remember that <u>**you must**</u> :

1. Have an interesting opening and a memorable ending

2. Have good characters, setting and plot

3. Build up suspense

4. Use dialogue – to move the story along

5. Use a variety of simple, compound and complex sentences

Plan your fiction writing:

PARAGRAPH 1	Write:
• Write an introduction to set the scene for your description. • Introduce the characters and the setting. • Introduce the plot.	• in **FIRST PERSON**, so you are the main character telling the story (using I or we) or • in **THIRD PERSON** (using he or she) as if you were a fly watching from the wall.
PARAGRAPH 2 • Develop the plot. • What might happen to trigger off a series of events? • Build up suspense.	**Remember:** • Use connectives or conjunctions: - *and or but (to join compound sentences)* - *or, so, if, when, while, after, before, because, unless, until, whereas, although (to join complex sentences)* - *use pronouns - who, which, whose, what, that* - *to link ideas use - firstly, later, therefore, on the other hand, at that moment, by this time, next, soon...* • Use a range of sentences – simple, compound and complex sentences • Use 'we' to identify with the reader. • Use 'you' for second person - in persuasive pieces and to speak directly to the reader.
PARAGRAPH 3 • Wind up your story with a good ending. In the resolution you will have solved all the problems. • It could be happy, sad, a cliff hanger (which leaves the reader to make up his or her own mind), or a moral ending • Have a memorable final sentence.	

The creepy **old** manor house was said to be *haunted* but Joshua didn't believe it. That is why he had come here – at night – **alone** and he was going in by himself. His friend had **dared** him to do it, but now it seemed a foolish idea.

Now write the story.

PLAN

Think about....

1. - Who are the characters?

    - Where is the setting?

    - What is the house like?

    - How does Joshua get in to the house?

2. - What happens when he is in the house? ...and after that?

(build up suspense, excitement, tension...)

3. - How does the story end?

    - Is there a moral lesson?

For these stories, use good adjectives, verbs and adverbs to conjure up an atmosphere of mystery. Use senses: what did he see, hear, smell, touch?

How do you feel when you are Scared?

What would it feel like in an empty <u>old</u> house?

What were those strange noises upstairs?

Who had come to the window of the empty house?

Whose footprints were in the garden?

How would you act if you thought you saw a ghostly thing?

The Creepy House

Joshua could hear his heart beating wildly, as he pushed the old door ajar. It creaked open. He held his breath for a moment. Now, he must step into that dark, dingy hallway. He wrestled with his emotions. It was only fear but he had never felt like this before. His legs were wobbly. Would they go on holding his body up? His hands were also shaking badly and his throat was dry. Then, he spoke aloud to himself. "What if... What if... the things people say are true? What if that ghostly figure at the window really does exist and that spectre is here now and I am going to...?"

A moment later, Joshua thought of the dare. He couldn't be beaten this time. It was important to summon every bit of courage and step over the threshold of the creepy house and confront whatever lay inside. There was an oppressively musty smell, but that was normal for houses of this age... wasn't it? He was inside – he'd made it this far. He blinked and looked around. The light was dim, but he could make out the shadow of a grandfather clock that had stopped at the stroke of midnight. There was also an old dresser, shrouded in a dusty cover, hung with cobwebs. A noise! What was it? He turned to run back, but the weather had changed outside. Torrents of rain were lashing down against the porch and the wind howled like a hungry dog. It rattled the shuttered windows. Another noise! It came from somewhere deep in the house. The sound of a voice - followed by footsteps treading lightly down the stairs. Oh no! Help me! What would happen now?

○ Write the ending paragraph of this story. Will it be a happy, sad, cliff hanger or moral ending?

Remember, when you describe the setting, use all the senses - see, hear, feel, smell, touch. Use good vocabulary.

....

....

....

....

....

....

....

....

....

....

....

....

....

....

Think imaginatively:

- Who do the footsteps belong to?
  (a cat, an old person, a ghost or a terrible...)

- Don't forget to build up suspense.

Here is a suggested ending:

Joshua was frozen to the spot. His hands were shaking; his teeth were chattering. He desperately wanted to run, but his legs would not move. Out of the corner of his eye, he saw a spider scuttle across the rotten floorboards and into a crack in the wall. "Be strong! Don't be scared," he muttered to himself – trying to find the courage to face this ghostly figure. The footsteps were getting louder and louder. Joshua grabbed the broken handle of a broom, discarded under the kitchen table, and turned to defend himself. However, it was not a ghost that appeared before him. It was a tiny withered up old lady that hobbled through the doorway. As their eyes met, Joshua thought – that will teach me never to believe in ghost stories.

This story ends on a cliff hanger. How could it be developed? Try rewriting the ending.

....
....
....
....
....
....
....
....
....
....
....
....

Now write your own ghost story.

....

....

....

....

....

....

....

....

....

....

....

....

....

....

....

....

....

....

....

....

....

....

....

....

....

Can you think of some words to describe wild settings?

Choose adjectives carefully. Be <u>selective</u> and choose the right one for the noun.

ADJECTIVE			NOUN
	barren	bare	land
		wild	wilderness
wild	windswept	desolate	moor
flat	open	exposed	plain
cold	chilly	dreary	weather
savage	untamed	harsh	wasteland
dark	gloomy	shadowy	corner
dreary	grey	stone	manor house
tangled	twisted	overgrown	shrubs
ram shackled	deserted	old	hall

WE FEEL:

fear	unease	worry	panic
anxiety	nervousness	dread	horror
fright	trepidation	apprehension	alarm
terror	distress	agitation	scared
terrified	upset	startled	shocked
traumatised	stunned	shaken	disturbed
distressed	distraught	troubled	petrified

Let's *empathise*. Have you ever imagined what it would be like to be an animal – a mouse maybe?

At the Stroke of Midnight

At the stroke of midnight, a pair of sharp yellow eyes stared out. They saw streaks of white lightning light up the sky like daybreak. The round ears twitched, as the thunder rolled and grumbled in the distance. The trees trembled because they couldn't sleep. Mouse shivered. There was a chill in the night air. Nervously, he watched the sky for the shadow of a predator swooping across the moors. The coast was clear, so he crept out into the depths of the night – a dark and dangerous night. As he moved swiftly under the cover of the dense, dark vegetation of the flower border, fluttering bats darted to and fro across the lawn, snapping gnats in their sharp jaws.

Ten minutes later, the mouse still fought his way, like a hero, through the tangling weeds that wound and twisted through the plants. His little, furry body was scratched and torn by sharp thorns, but, he was a mouse on a mission and he must go on. He ventured forward, until he came to the part of the garden, where the flower bed gave way to the extensive lawn, that lay before the house. There it was, the house of horrors, which stood looking down on him menacingly. Its crumbling stonewalls and dark panes of lattice glass seemed to frown, but he must go on and meet the challenge. Keeping in the shadows, he scampered up the dusty footpath to the step and sniffed the creaking door that stood ajar and then… his heart pounding, he pushed through the smallest gap and stood in the dark, silent, musty hall way. All in the space of a second, his eyes made out the shape of dusty furnishings, shrouded in sheets: an old chair, a table and veils of white cobwebs which hung like ghostly phantoms from the ceiling. But, more than this, a hideous white monster appeared in front of him. It fixed its ferocious gaze on him. In an instant, its mouth opened wide, revealing a row of sharp canine teeth, its claws extended and it pounced. Mouse froze. Was his fate sealed?

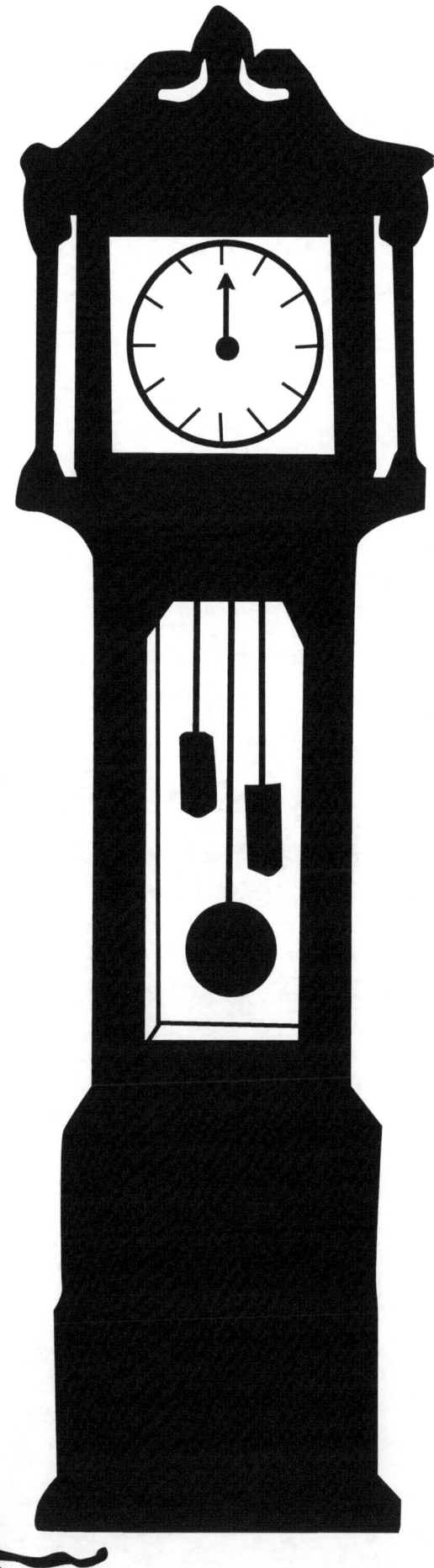

In the flash of a second, mouse had realised the peril he was in – but he did not give up easily. With one swift movement he escaped the jaws of the ghostly cat. He summoned up all his strength to pull away from the creature's deadly grip. Then he fled at great speed through the crack in the door, back to the dusty step. After this, he scurried back – back – back along the footpath in the moonlight at such speed. The fear made his eyes as red as blood. He kept running until he came to the safety of the tangled undergrowth. There, he paused to catch his breath. When he had recovered a bit, he ran on, over the twisty roots, of the lazy trees that snored above him. As dawn approached, the feeble sun

prepared to creep up. Back at the safety of his own home, he collapsed on the bed, his tail drooping with exhaustion. Closing his eyes, he tried to block out the horrors of the night. Although, he had escaped, the terrifying image of the ghostly cat kept coming back to him. He had seen it with his own eyes and he could report back and no one could ever say that he hadn't accepted the challenge and overcome his own fear.

○ Make a list of interesting verbs, adverbs, nouns and adjectives in the story.

Can you find any similes or metaphors?
Can you find any examples of personification?

Can you write your own version of the story?

....

....

....

....

....

....

....

....

....

....

....

....

....

....

....

....

....

....

....

....

....

....

....

....

A new attraction at the fair is opening called:

Little House of HORRORS

Come and be *terrified* at the little House of Horrors. Bring the family for a *spine* chilling <u>adventure</u> that you won't forget!

Write a **spooky spine, chilling** advertisement to persuade families to come and have some fearful fun as they wander round this spooky place.

You could **experiment** with <u>*different*</u> sorts of **font** or writing to grab the reader's attention.

Use the words on the vocabulary pages to help you create an absolutely amazing **atmosphere** - that will <u>*make every hair stand on end*</u>.

Can you think of any more **_spooky_** words and phrases?

spine chilling spectres	**terrifying beasts**	ghastly ghouls
ghostly phantoms	witch riding on a broomstick	layers of white cobwebs
danger lurking round every corner	screeching owls	rusty lock
bubbling cauldron	spooky spiders scuttling	_shivering_
book of spells	**_spine tingling_**	spooky
goose bumps	lurking in the dark	**black fluttering bats**
clicking bones	squeamish	heart-pounding
heart-racing	_bony skeletons_	brittle bones
jingling joints	bones clicking	**black cat**
slamming door	creaking floor boards	howling wind
haunted house	bad wizard	blood sucking vampires
as pale as death	**_ware wolves howling_**	blood curdling screams

The best story I know was called the *Midnight Express train*... I don't even remember the name of the author, but it was so exciting that I couldn't put it down. It was late at night. The streets lights were casting shadows across my room. I was reading under the covers to avoid annoying my parents. The pages were turning faster and faster as the events unfolded before my tired eyes. Then, a peculiar sensation came upon me – the warmth of my cosy quilt was replaced by the chill of the night air. I was being transported to another place far, far away.

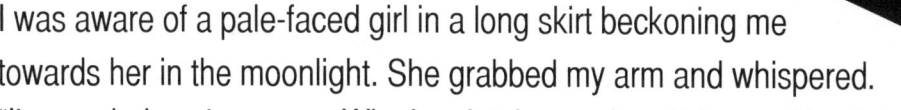

I was aware of a pale-faced girl in a long skirt beckoning me towards her in the moonlight. She grabbed my arm and whispered.
"I'm so glad you've come. Why has it taken so long?' I stared back into her tear stained eyes.
"What's up?" I stammered.
"It's Jack, he's in a bad way," she replied. Follow me quickly. As I looked around I saw we were on the edge of a small wood. She led me across uneven ground, clambering over protruding trees, dodging around shrubs and scraping our knees on sharp twigs. Then we were descending down a steep slope, to a single rail track.
"Hurry," she pleaded gently. She led the way into a tunnel. It was pitch black. My heart had never beaten so fast. Then I heard the cry.
"Help me! Please help me!"

I held my breath. I didn't know what to expect there in the darkness. Then a small hand grabbed mine. A boy's voice groaned in pain. He was hurt. Between us we managed to lift the injured child and slowly made our way back to the entrance of the tunnel. It was just in time. As we collapsed exhausted, on the damp grass of the embankment, a great roaring sound grew louder and louder and a huge old-fashioned steam train thundered past at top speed. Then we were surrounded by a group of men. They were mumbling.
"Thank goodness you're alive." The girl was sobbing and speaking very fast.
"Jack went in to get Rover. He was chasing a rabbit and he fell." As she spoke, the little boy gripped my hand hard – harder – and harder. I awoke with a start and sat up in my bed. I noticed my book had fallen open and on a scrap of paper was written,

'Thank you for saving my brother'.

Now write your own story about a strange dream you had at midnight, or alternatively an adventure you had when you went out at midnight.

....

....

....

....

....

....

....

....

....

....

....

....

....

....

....

....

....

....

....

....

....

....

....

....

....

....

....

....

....

....

....

....

- Who were you with? (character)

Where did you go? (setting)

Why? (plot)

What happened next? ... and after that?

Remember to build up suspense.

How did it end?

The following article appeared in 'Wiz' magazine – aimed at all 'SPOOKY things' that go bump in the night. Can the organisers PERSUADE you to come?

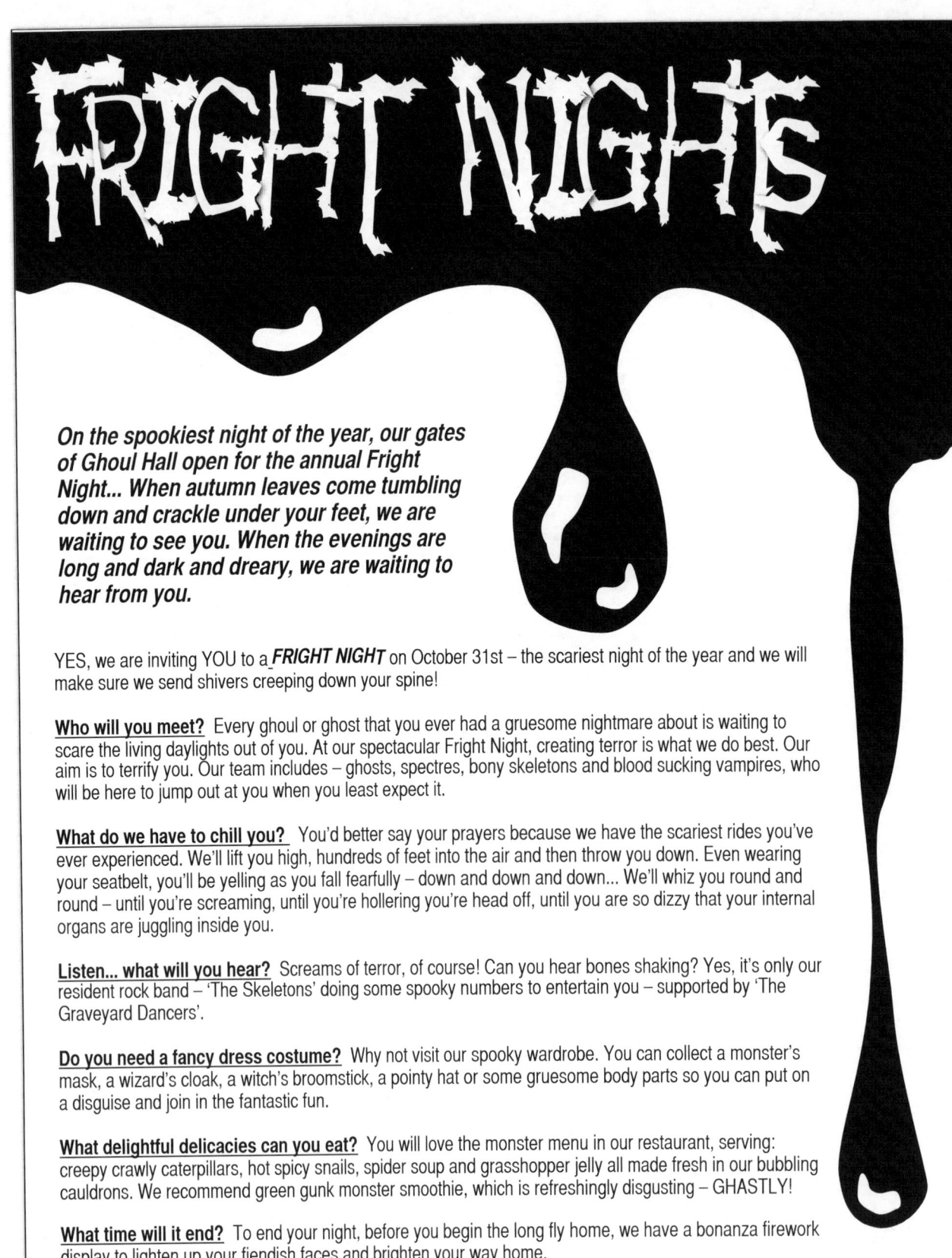

FRIGHT NIGHTS

On the spookiest night of the year, our gates of Ghoul Hall open for the annual Fright Night... When autumn leaves come tumbling down and crackle under your feet, we are waiting to see you. When the evenings are long and dark and dreary, we are waiting to hear from you.

YES, we are inviting YOU to a **FRIGHT NIGHT** on October 31st – the scariest night of the year and we will make sure we send shivers creeping down your spine!

Who will you meet? Every ghoul or ghost that you ever had a gruesome nightmare about is waiting to scare the living daylights out of you. At our spectacular Fright Night, creating terror is what we do best. Our aim is to terrify you. Our team includes – ghosts, spectres, bony skeletons and blood sucking vampires, who will be here to jump out at you when you least expect it.

What do we have to chill you? You'd better say your prayers because we have the scariest rides you've ever experienced. We'll lift you high, hundreds of feet into the air and then throw you down. Even wearing your seatbelt, you'll be yelling as you fall fearfully – down and down and down... We'll whiz you round and round – until you're screaming, until you're hollering you're head off, until you are so dizzy that your internal organs are juggling inside you.

Listen... what will you hear? Screams of terror, of course! Can you hear bones shaking? Yes, it's only our resident rock band – 'The Skeletons' doing some spooky numbers to entertain you – supported by 'The Graveyard Dancers'.

Do you need a fancy dress costume? Why not visit our spooky wardrobe. You can collect a monster's mask, a wizard's cloak, a witch's broomstick, a pointy hat or some gruesome body parts so you can put on a disguise and join in the fantastic fun.

What delightful delicacies can you eat? You will love the monster menu in our restaurant, serving: creepy crawly caterpillars, hot spicy snails, spider soup and grasshopper jelly all made fresh in our bubbling cauldrons. We recommend green gunk monster smoothie, which is refreshingly disgusting – GHASTLY!

What time will it end? To end your night, before you begin the long fly home, we have a bonanza firework display to lighten up your fiendish faces and brighten your way home.

Whether you're a wicked witch, an evil wizard or just a ghostly ghoul, come to a 'Fright Night' and we'll show you just how much we hate you.

Is white rat _not_ convinced?

Don't go to the ball
At spooky Ghoul Hall.

On such a dark night,
It will give you a fright.

Your resident host
Is only a ghost.

His guests: evil creatures
With hideous features.

Don't be whizzed round,
Keep your feet on the ground.

The rides make you scream,
It will be like a bad dream.

And what is the prize
For the best disguise?

It's grasshopper jelly -
That's bad for your belly.

Be warned: Keep a light,
A pumpkin burning bright.

And watch over your gate,
Until it's quite late.

Then, cover your ears,
To block out your fears.

Stay peaceful and glad,
Not terrified and sad.

**Can you find any
rhyming couplets?**

Imagine you are a ghostly ghoul.

Recount a visit to 'Fright Night'.

On the spookiest night of the year...

I went to ....

.... at .... on ...

....

Halloween is on 31st October, the day before the Christian festival of All Saints Day. It is a tradition to burn pumpkin lanterns until midnight, to protect homes from any evil. Some children dress up in costumes and go 'tricking and treating' – that is calling at doors to receive sweets or money or to play a trick. Some people have Halloween parties and dress up as scary creatures. Others have light parties.

The event got started...

- *at night fall*
- *as darkness fell.*
- *when all good folk are tucked up in their beds.*

The gruesome fright team included...

- *ghosts.*
- *zombies.*
- *vampires.*
- *werewolves.*

They were terrifying between...

- *they shrieked and howled.*
- *jumped out on me.*
- *they cackled.*

First, I went to the spooky wardrobe where I..

- *hired*
- *bought*
- *collected*

- *a monster's mask*
- *a wizard's cloak*
- *a witch's broomstick*

Next, I experienced terror on the rides which...

- *lifted me high.*
- *threw me down.*
- *whizzed me round.*

The scariest ride was...

-    ....

I found my/myself...

- *screaming.*
- *yelling.*
- *dizzy.*
- *hollering my head off.*
- *insides juggled together.*

Rock band 'The Graveyard Diggers' were...

- *awesome,*
- *amazing performers,*
- *entertaining,*
- *filled us with trepidation,*

because they...

- *clinked their bones.*
- *nailed it.*
- *ought to be on the Z Factor.*

The worst thing was the meal in the
restaurant, which consisted of...

- *creepy crawly caterpillar eye balls.*
- *grass hopper jelly.*
- *hot spicy snails.*

It was suitably...

- *disgusting!*
- *Yuk!*
- *Vile!*

Was it worth firing up my
broomstick for the event...

- *I loved it because...*
- *I hated it because...*

Would you tell your friends to go next year?.

- *Yes, because it is so much fun. I had a wonderful time.*
- *No, because it is very scary. It is dark and dangerous.*

Rock band '*The Graveyard Diggers*' backed by '*The Spooky Skeletons*' dance troupe audition on...

The Z<u>Factor</u>

What do the judges think?

Write some comments from the judges?

....	....	....

Plan your own <u>FANCY DRESS</u> party
What would you include?

What would you dress up as?

(you could choose a character from a book)

What games would you play?

What food would you serve?

What music would you play?

What decorations would you put up?

Apple bobbing is a traditional Halloween game. You have to lift an apple with your teeth from a bucket of water.

THE DAILY NEWS

ALL ABOUT THE BIG WORLD WE LIVE IN

Ghouls, Ghosts, Wizards and Witches turned out for Ghoul Hall's annual 'Fright Night!'

EXCLUSIVE: Ghostly face seen at the window of Deathly Grange.

A *FRIGHTFUL* Night Out

A spine chilling night; not for the faint hearted.

By Anya Smith

At nightfall on the spookiest night of the year, Ghoul Hall creaked open its gates, for its annual 'Fright Night'. Hundreds of ghosts, ghouls, witches and wizards came to...

The 'Fright Night' aimed to...
The rides were extra scary this year. especially the...

The most weird and wonderful costume award was won by... who wore...

'The Skeletons', a rock band, performed some of their hits called...

and dance troupe 'The Spooky Bones' wowed the audience with their...

The 'ghastly' menu was as disgusting as ever featuring...

Picture: FRIGHT NIGHT OUT

The night drew to an end with a bonanza firework extravaganza, which was...

Wizard ... screamed shrilly, "It was awesome fun because..."

Miss... cackled hysterically, "It was a bone chilling evening..."

The evening revelries ended sharply at midnight, as guests departed into the night. As the pumpkin lanterns burnt brightly - good had overcome evil.

THE DAILY NEWS

ALL ABOUT THE BIG WORLD WE LIVE IN

....

....

....

....

....

....

A Frightful Night Out

....

....

By ....

....

....

....

....

....

....

....

....

....

....

....

....

....

....

Picture: ....

....

....

....

....

....

....

....

....

....

....

....